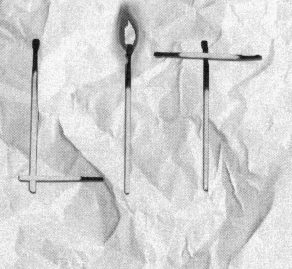

SPOKEN-WORD ANTHOLOGY
OF IDENTITY AND LOVE

S H E L B Y   B I R C H

LIT

Shelby Birch

Library of Congress Control Number:		2017900892
ISBN:	Hardcover	978-1-5245-7741-4
	Softcover	978-1-5245-7742-1
	eBook	978-1-5245-7743-8

To order additional copies of this book, contact:
Xlibris
1-888-795-4274
www.Xlibris.com
Orders@Xlibris.com
755541

Dedicated
To Tifanny, Takai, Mom and Dad, and Blu Bailey
To the little black girl who is still trying to find her voice
To the woman who forgot she was enough
To the Comets who have lit my sky, heart and pen

Contents

Foreword ix

Flame

Burnt

Foreword

Nikki, Maya, Sonia, Angela, Zora, all brilliant black female poets. All whose writing made a difference and changed the landscape of the African cultural forms in America and around the world. The rhythmic beat of their words show their connection to their African ancestors, who used Ring Shouts, Juba dance, lining of hymns, etc. to communicate as a vital part of the African culture. Both Shakespeare and John Milton use iambic-pentameter as a basis for their poetry, which dictates a certain rhythm. Today's generation uses a syncopated rhythm in an African cultural form called spoken word poetry to express their thoughts.

Along comes Shelby Birch, a brilliant young black woman 'Spitting' spoken word poetry like no other. Shelby has a superb command of the English language and the metaphors she uses to express herself are sometimes too powerful to be heard only once. So as the young generation hollers, 'rewind', is heard a lot. In my thirty plus years as an entertainment professional and twenty plus as a professor, I have worked with some of the best, and based on my experience, Shelby fits into that category as a spoken word artist, a poet. She is very good at what she does.

I first met Shelby when she came to me as a college freshman, and asked me to be the faculty advisor for a spoken word group she wanted to start on campus called "Project: Student Poetry Initiating Thought" (Project: SPIT). Her leadership skills and ability to network turned Project: SPIT into one of the most popular groups on campus, with 300 attendees, winning the 2013-2014 New Organization of the Year, and the 2015 Organization of the Year award at the University of Central Florida. In 2015 their slam team ranked 5th out of 65 teams at College Unions Poetry Slam Invitational (CUPSI), their first international competition. I've seen her perform at the International Zora Neale Hurston Festival of the Arts, in front of live audiences from all over the U.S. receiving standing ovations.

While in school, she volunteered at Harbor House, Habitat For Humanity, Second Harvest Food Bank, The Write and mentored students in Orange County Public Schools in poetry. On campus she served on executive boards for organizations such as Project: SPIT, John T. Washington Honor Society, Orientation Team, President's Leadership Council, Alpha Kappa Psi Professional Business Fraternity, and she is a proud member of Delta Sigma Theta Sorority, Inc. The list goes on.

Not only is *Lit* a compelling exposé of life experiences through anthological spoken word poetry, but it is a breathtaking book to read. We see an individual through her cultural legacy, open up her intellect and her emotions. This book is a work of art. I am sure you will find some experiences you can relate to. I did, and we are generations apart.

Nikki, Maya, Sonia, Angela, Zora and now **Shelby!**

Anthony B. Major
University of Central Florida, UCF
Associate Professor, Film/SVAD
Director of Africana Studies & Zora Neale Hurston Institute for Documentary Studies.

Light

[lahyt]

Noun

1. ~~Something that makes things visible or affords illumination:~~
2. **The radiance or illumination from a particular source.**

Lit

[lit]

Verb

1. ~~A simple past tense and past participle of light†.~~

Adjective

1. *~~Slang.~~* ~~Under the influence of liquor or narcotics; intoxicated (usually followed by~~ *~~up~~*~~).~~
2. ~~When something is turned up or popping.~~
3. **Something that is amazing in any sense.**
4. ~~The act of which a person is excited, or hype due to an upcoming event.~~

Lit [lit]

Noun. Adjective.

The radiance or illumination from a particular source. Something that is amazing in any sense.

Warning

Contains highly flammable content. Hazardous to closed minds and negative energies. May cause severe internal self-reflection or burn marks from setting your soul on fire. Side effects may include: headaches from constant thought provocation, insomnia or "wokeness," and random sudden outbursts of "yasssss!" if read in public spaces.

If you can't take the heat, get out of the book.

Flame

[fleym]

Noun

1. ~~Burning gas or vapor, as from wood or coal that is undergoing combustion; a portion of ignited gas or vapor.~~
2. ~~Any flame like condition; glow; inflamed condition.~~
3. ~~Brilliant light; scintillating luster.~~
4. **Intense ardor, zeal, or passion.**

Verb (used without object), **flamed, flaming.**

5. ~~To burn with a flame or flames; burst into flames; blaze.~~
6. ~~To glow like flame; shine brilliantly; flash.~~
7. **To burn or burst forth with strong emotion; break into open anger, indignation, etc.**
8. ~~Computer Slang. To post an angry, critical, or disparaging electronic message, as an online comment.~~

Flame [fleym]

Noun. Verb.

Intense ardor, zeal or passion. To burn or burst forth with strong emotion; break into open anger, indignation, etc.

Black Girl
(22 years old)

Black girl

With narrow or wide hips
With nose wide like rubber band meadows stretching across
    face
And flat like squished gum on sidewalks they kill black
    bodies on
You've held your breath for too long
Forgot to wake up to smell the garden that lingers in your
    scent
Your fragrance cannot be bottled, branded nor bought
Roses gossip on their vines
Compete with your beauty because you seem to bloom and
    bouquet better
They ask to grow from your seeds so they can have roots as
    kinky and deep as yours

But you place your worth in hands who know not how to
    handle you
Who prick themselves but blame your thorns for being there
They guilt you for being too strong

They guilt you for being too sharp
Even in the workplace and in wit
They will treat you like shit
They will tell you to go fuck yourself
They will tell you that you're unpretty

And you will believe that you're unpretty.

You will try to fuck others to remind yourself of your worth
That maybe it's found in the womb of an orgasm
And as they play archeologist
They will try to dig into you and excavate your walls hoping
    they will find you
Instead they will find themselves
Because somehow,
You think spreading yourself will open up lines closer to the
    god you worship in others
The god you think exists in bodies you lay with in the grave
    of your bed
The skeletons in your closet are found underneath your skin
How you hold secrets in your sheets
You let them between your legs
You've mistaken the location of your heart for your vagina
The attention you're dying for is killing your self esteem

Black girl

With skin as rich as soil
You've let them call you manure
You've forgotten that you got Harlem Renaissance for a mind
And Civil Rights for fists
I saw Nina Simone playing on the piano keys of your teeth
    when you smiled the other day

But Black girl

Why have you neglected to write your poetry?
Do you feel that you're not worth the words?
Your name alone has improved English language
Challenged French to sound more romantic
For you have wooed Shakespearians and twisted tongues to
    command better diction when speaking of your presence
Are you afraid at how beautiful you may sound that parallels
    the human gaze?
Are you afraid that it could be accurate?

Or are you afraid that you just can't see it?

With skin as dark as night
With soul as light as day
You hold an equinox in your eyes
You hold earthquake in your walk
Yet, you flood your mind with thoughts that destroy your
    being
You beat yourself down before the police can
Afraid to bleach your skin yet you bleach your confidence

Black girl

Are tired of just being … *black girl*?
When will you have strength to speak your name?
Speak your name!
Speak your beautiful name

When will you realize that the love you've been looking for
Is only found within
Yourself

Oreo
(17 years old)

They called me an Oreo
Ya know,
Black on the outside but white on the inside
To some double stuffed with the stuff my people hate me for
So they choose to crunch my esteem into pieces

Nestle left me human
Straight outta factory, they branded me
My people tried to turn me inside out to rid me out of my
    insides
But how dare you
Outsiders looking in
Invite your insults
Call me out of my name and belittle me into an object!

I turned out to be the poster child for what a black person
    wasn't supposed to be
A cookie
But don't you remember our ancestors came in packages, too?

Savages thrown into fielded factories
To be me manufactured
To please the tongues of our masters
They snacked on privilege while *we* starved from prejudice
It was distasteful to be seen or heard
Why do Black people hate me for sounding so good?
They say my tongue is tainted
I sound like "Becky" or "Kaitlyn"
It must be proper to speak improper English?
I derived my diction from dictionaries
I guess Webster was bullied as a child, too

Society expects me to embody the bodies of lost somebodies
    we find bodied in the ghetto's mentality
I'm forced to lose my character and become one
Bonqui-qui and shanay-nay say I'll earn my black pass this
    way
Are you kidding me?
They'd rather ride in black caskets and be out-casted into
    stereotypes and statistics
They'd rather be Jordan than cross the Jordan
They'd rather have Jordans than have sense

Although they called me a cookie
I knew they crunched, chewed and swallowed their jealousy
    they had toward me

I lingered in their tracheas
I echoed my wind to pipe down demons destroying the lost
    language of gullah they long to speak
But I constantly got blamed and undeservingly shamed
It all sounded the same,
"You ain't black enough"
"You a confused black girl"
"Why do you act so white?"
Mimicked my oh my goshes
Rained on my happiness as they stepped in the puddles of my
    identity crisis in their ignorant goulashes

I thought acting a color was impossible
But if I started acting orange then I guess purple would start
    hating on me, too
I remember when I was colorblind
Now I'm blinded by color

Jim crows flew to rainbows
Now there is racism across the spectrum, the nation
Society scratched me with its acrylic nail and made me see
the world for what it is
Segregated

We are a population that is still separated within our own
races
Erase it
Accept me for who I am.

For anyone trying to prove themselves to themselves or within
their own culture
Stop trying
I did a long time ago
It's time to take on the world and show them what you're
about
And for the ones who still dare to compare me to an Oreo
Or a Chips Ahoy
Or a Vanilla Wafer…

I hope this poem leaves a bad taste in your mouth.

Identity Part 1: Strikes

I already have three strikes against me:

Black.
Woman.
And Awkward.

On Black Hair

The most beautiful thing about black hair is its versatility.
We are able to transform our hair into limitless
creations that challenge and change the discourse of
the beauty ideal. We are constantly evolutionizing and
revolutionizing our hair by establishing the latest trends
that is mimicked then appropriated by popular culture.

Black hair is ALWAYS good hair
And should not be viewed as anything less.

I Do Not Dread My Dreads
(19 years old)

"Shelby, you need to cut those dreads and put weave back in.
Your hair looks horrible and you look like a boy." – *Assholes*

This poem is dedicated to people like me
Who tend to forget who and where they come from

I've learned that regret is nothing but an insecurity and fear
    in a self-made decision that was never questioned nor
    challenged
So I do not regret the day that it happened
The day I made my way to the salon
    To go on
    And loc my hair

I do not dread my dreads
I dread your rejection

As if the reflection I see in the mirror of our skins,
Or the curl in our roots,
Has no connection to the beauty that was once chained and
    noosed by skins of our self-esteem?

We come from queens with the same curl patterns that held
　　cotton fields in their hairs and spirituals at the base laced
　　in lyrics
We share the same parts in our hair that opened the pages of
　　the untold parts of our stories
Yet, I am labeled un-pretty
Because I rock locs instead of rocks concoct'd into creamy
　　crack and Remy

I do not dread my dreads
I dread your unacceptance

I never liked to get burned by perms
I groaned at combs
I'd rather bleed blood than bleed product
Straighten my attitude before I straighten my new growth
But I'm constantly reminded:

"Guuurrrllll, when your hair grows out, then that's when
　　you'll be pretty!" – *Friends who try to give me hope*
"You're just in the ugly phase of the process!" – *Friends who
　　fail at giving me hope*
"I only like girls with long hair." - *Assholes*

But the rate of hair growth is about 1/2 an inch per month
Which equates to 6 inches per year
So the timeframe in which I will regain my beauty will be….
Not now.
As if the twist of your head depends on the length of my
    twists

But I do not dread my dreads for they are holy

For every Rastafari who hails Selassie
For every Zendaya who spat patchouli oil and weed back into
    the eyes of the media
For every Sampson who escaped a Delilah

Every inch that is grown is a prayer uplifted and a blessing
    bestowed
Each dread is a request for my happiness
Each loc is God's protection
Each nap puts my demons to sleep
Why worship a god in a perm box when a God grows from
    my head in curly knots

I do not dread my dreads
I dread your judgment

They said in the real world,
"Dreadlocs will dead bolt your future"
But try telling that to Toni Morrison, Whoopi Goldberg or
    Lauryn Hill
For every dread head who's been deemed dreadful
For every woman who hides behind the weaves and hats to
    cover the naps
This is for you

This hairstyle is only by preference
But I'm not asking for acceptance
I'm demanding respect
You don't have to love them
But if you're still hatin' on them…

Then you can suck them.

But before you judge them
Remember that we come from the same people who took
    pride in the way I choose to wear my hair today
I am not changing myself for anyone
Because I do not dread my dreads

Permission

"May I touch your hair?"
Thanks for asking permission!
Answer is still no.

Identity Part 2: Percentages

97% IDGAF
2% Well…maybe I do
1% Nah.

Grandma's Red Sauce

Grandma made pasta when there was no more chicken left to
    fry
Replaced Africa with Italy in those hands
Though she's never been overseas
At 79
Her taste buds have traveled to lands of oregano and basil
She measured thyme perfectly
Befriended rosemary with some sage glittering in her eyes
She found a getaway in cooking
And her red sauce always took me along for a ride
Red
The color of passion
Like in her last marriage
And the color of anger
Like in her last divorce
I tasted her story on my tongue
Grandma's red sauce
Dressed pasta like dressing her children before they went to
    school
Reminded me what it's like to be black and woman
To be Italian Chef
Yet ~~American~~ slave
To be saucy and sassy
To be well traveled in the confines of a kitchen
To have opportunity lay within recipes found at the bottom of
    pots
I loved Grandma's red sauce
Bravissimo to the chef

Identity Part 3: "Describe Yourself"

I'm a cross between an intellectual and a trap queen.

Identity Part 4: The Clap Back

Him: Your eyebrows aren't fleeky today.
Me: Neither is your ambition or bank account,
but that's none of my business.
Him: *struggles to collect jaw and entire
manhood off the ground*

Backbone
(19 years old)

Women are the backbone of the world
And mama ain't raised no fools
It's time to receive the credit where credit is due
It's been passed notice
For we've been passed and gone un-noticed for the burdens
    we bury on our backs;
For the bruises bestowed on our bones
We've been holding y'all up
By holding it down
We are the uncrowned queens of the universe
Watch our thrones and behold the truth
Bless our feet that carried your world in the depths of our
    wombs
We've been cooking the nation in the pots of our bellies and
    humanity has never tasted so good

Now is the time to take back our titles and restore our
    queen-doms
Girl power is an understatement when womanhood breaks the
    bonds from misogyny into freedom

We are the ladies who sang the blues
The eyes who were watching God
The figurative language in your poetry
We hold the power of a population in our ovaries
Brought breath to the lungs
Stood by our men even if it meant standing by ourselves
Put the suffer in Suffrage and turned it into a movement
Ask any man to make change in a pencil skirt and stilettos
    and see if he can do it
I think not
We are the Coretta Scotts who are still looking for our Kings
    to bring us up another notch

We women have already claimed our spots in history

But history may not claim us back
Maybe we have some bones to pick
But when you're too busy being a backbone to the weak and
    spineless, getting recognition is irrelevant
It's time to reinvent the concept of a woman
Redefine the perimeters mankind has boxed us in
We've been thinking outside the Crayola box for far too long
Color in some details with female
We've paid our dues
We walk that walk
We talk that talk
We sure look good doing both

Examine our skeletons and see that our bones are stronger
    than steel;
We are not easily broken
We bend our backs to put food on tables
Or bend our backs as tables if there are none to begin with
If we are losing in war
We pull pieces of vertebrae from our spine to put in a barrel
    of a gun as ammunition

We use our backbones as crosses to place Jesus on there
To remind us that he still lives within us

We put meaning back into sacrifice
And put sacrifice back into prospective
And waking up every day may be tough knowing that the
    world is already against us
But remember…
A man might be the head
But a woman will always be the neck
A man might be the head
But the woman will always be the neck
To hold you up
And to hold you down
We might be living in a man's world
But it ain't nothin' without a woman

We've got one hell of a job
We are the backbones of planet Earth
Now we deserve credit where credit is due
Because everyone should know a woman's true worth

Dear Heroine
(21 years old)

Dear Heroine,
Please tell me what it's like
To be too much woman for a body that couldn't hold the depth
and beauty that you possessed
To have seen so much war from a bedside that would bring
Hercules to his knees
And humble Zeus to human

Please tell me what it's like
To be overflowing with heaven in your smile though you were
going through hell
Trapped in a jail where justice just sat to watch you wither
away
You never acknowledged your disease as a cell block
But rather a ship that would sail in oceans toward freedom
Your face reflected in waters as we reflected on your
memories in your hurricane season
Poseidon welcomed our tears when we would cry for you
But used them in his tides to push you toward God

Dear Heroine
We couldn't help but to be salty

But you refused to let us throw it in our wounds
You told us to use it to season our bitterness so we can taste a
    new day
To seize the moment when you treaded seas to see the other
    side

Dear Heroine
Please tell me what it's like to hold a thousand splendid suns
    in your eyes
Just to supernova toward Jesus
To be so benign when your enemy was malignant toward you
To sit comfortably in stages that told the greatest story ever
    made
But scared the greatest actors to portray
Your children memorized its lines
Unfortunately knew how the story would end
Prayed for a plot twist or miracle
But understand that you stand a heroine as you martyred your
    life so they could have a story to tell
Let your name be legend
Let your name be folklore
Lure folks into remembering your legacy

Dear Heroine
Even your name told us to make sense from this change going
    on in your life

You broke our hearts and emptied our pockets
We wish you could've stayed a quarter of a time longer
If I had a nickel every time we mourned we'd be millionaires
But as we worried about your health
You kept multiplying your wealth
Getting richer as you won the game with every card that you
    were dealt
And although the cancer couldn't be flushed
You kept a full house of family as you kept your poker face
    still
Didn't want us to fold under pressure in this game you never
    wanted to play
But you won in eternity Dear Heroine
To sit alongside a King with a royal flush of Holy Spirit
Dear Heroine
I know your favorite color is purple, but would you consider
    pink for just one month?
It's the color of your victory flag that your family waves
    everyday
Not to surrender
But to remember that you still live on
Please continue to sing your song
So that we can continue to find you as we continue to find a
    cure to breast cancer

Dear Heroine
I know this poem may be too late
Because you left us too soon
But if I had a penny for every beautiful prayer you sent up
For every smile you showered on a stranger
For every hug you gave to your sisters
For every clap you gave to give God praise
For every moment you felt like giving up but remembered you
    were already saved
For every kiss you gave your children goodnight…..
Then I would be a millionaire

Dear Heroine,
Please tell me what it's like
To be too much woman for a body that couldn't hold the depth
    and beauty that you possessed
Breast cancer did not defeat you
But rather released you
And I'm so happy
That your story will forever live on

Sincerely,
Shelby

Catharsis

I see that you've been broken
Your smile says it all
Beautiful, yet forced
As if it hurts to look that gorgeous
Who made you feel anything less than glorious?
Remember conversing with Aphrodite?
Composing symphonies with Bach?
Giggling with Galileo?
Yet, tears Niagara Fall your cheeks
Your insecurities,
A leaking faucet
Every ounce of you drips
Maybe that's why you're drained everyday
I know it hurts sometimes
To be burdened with beauty and brilliance
Or with shit that threatens your existence
But I am knapsack,
Baggage claim and truck
Unload your pain unto me,
Without giving any fucks
We'll thrive on new memories of happiness and trust
Jive. Gyrate. Dance and shuck
Get high on freedom and get drunk on love
Shout hallelujahs to the angels above
Cherish everything as is and forget every hurt there ever was

3am (Starbucks is Closed)
(21 years old)

It is 3am
And Starbucks is closed
So I guess I'll make this room my coffee shop
An open mic with just my name on the list
I've invited my demons to spectate
To watch me choke on this pillow I named microphone
Where I've tried suffocating my poetry
I've spent nights inking my ugly in bed sheets and comforters
But there's no comforting in covers that wrap these stains in
    thoughts
These thoughts
Tend to leak out of my imagination on accident
I have trouble holding them in like bad bladders
Call my nightmares bed wetter
Call them childish
But I lay comfortable in them while playing Russian roulette
    with depression as the bullet
My angst holds the gun
My anxiety seduces my fingers to cock back and bang my
    brain with thoughts that run marathons
I hold onto depression like last goodbyes
It just never wants to leave

                        I just wish Starbucks was open at 3am
            But the only thing open are these cuts from digging this pen
                    into the skin of this notebook, wishing it was mine
                            I don't know why I'm troubled at night

Why bed bugs bug my bed and mind
Why insomnia is the seductress that fucks with my peace of
mind
She lingers in my bosom
Hoping I can hold onto her a little bit longer
Ya know, it's hard breaking up with someone you've been in a
relationship with for years
Depression was there for everything
I mean, together we cried rivers in my mattress that
swallowed us whole while drowning in misery
Titanic'd its way into my heart
It's hard getting out of bed when your lover anchors your
motivation to seafloors of worry and fear
I'm just in too deep at this point

It is 3am
And Starbucks is *still* closed
Like my heart.
But unlike my legs
Like my mind.
But unlike my mouth
Trapped in comfort zones that I can't escape
I thought this bedroom was a coffee shop
But there's only loneliness brewing in my mind
Barista's look like bad memories
I've overdosed on coffee, caffeine and constant conversation
with grief
I just want to go to sleep
I don't write poems anymore
I write nightmares in rhyme schemes that people seem to snap for

It is 3am
And Starbucks is *still* closed
And I wish my room wasn't a coffee shop
I wish it wasn't an open mic
I just wish I could sleep
I just wish I could go to sleep
I just want to go to sleep

It is 7am
And Starbucks is *now* open…
But I think I'll stay in bed today.
I'll get coffee another time.
I'll choose to lay in bed with my lover, depression, who
    welcomes my fear into our home we call bedroom
Where I'll continue to stain these thoughts in our sheets.

Identity Part 5: Grown Up

"Shelby, what do you want to be when you grow up?"

7 years old: "White"
7 years old: "Barbie"
8 years old: "An archeologist"
8 years old: "A mommy"
9 years old: "A doctor"
10 years old: "Black"
11 years old: "A lawyer"
11 years old: "A police officer"
14 years old: "A wedding planner"
14 years old: "Loved"
15 years old: "A chef"
15 years old: "Noticed"
15 years old: "Popular"
15 years old: "Loved"

16 years old: "Grown"

16 years old: "Beautiful"

16 years old: "Enough"

16 years old: "Loved"

17 years old: "Dead"

17 years old: ~~A poet~~ "In love"

17 years old: ~~A poet~~ "Loved…by somebody"

18 years old: ~~A poet~~ "A wife"

18 years old: ~~A poet~~ "Definitely not a wife"

18 years old: ~~A poet~~ "Alone"

18 years old: ~~A poet~~ "Loved…by anybody"

20 years old: ~~A poet~~ "Happy"

20 years old: ~~A poet~~ "Taken Serious"

20 Years old: ~~A poet~~ "Myself"

20 years old: ~~A poet~~ "Alive"

20 years old: ~~A poet~~ "Loved…by whoever"

21 years old: ~~A poet~~ "I don't know"

21 years old: ~~A poet~~ "I don't know"

21 years old: ~~A poet~~ "I don't know"

21 years old: ~~A poet~~ ~~"Loved…by you"~~

22 years old: A poet. Loved by myself

Lethal Weapon

Let your smile claw at your troubles
Let your passion be a bullet to your worries
Let your joy slay your dream killers
Let your peace destroy those who oppress love everyday
Wear your happiness as your armor
Ready for war against the pain
That's what you call a lethal weapon
It was hard being fearless today
But I chose to be brave anyway

Lit

Don't ever forget that you are light
You are aurora and sun
You are luminous and bright
Moons may try to eclipse your shine
But supernova past them anyway

Don't ever forget that you are fire
You are flame and inferno
You are match and lighter
Hell hath no fury on the heat you emit
So burn beautiful, baby

Don't ever forget that you are light
Don't ever forget that you are fire
You are radiant in the mind
You are blazing in your brilliance
Don't ever forget, that you are lit

For Sakena, Tifanny, Curtis, Talia and You (Your Poem)
(20 years old)

I want to let you know that it's going to be okay
Even if you feel like it's not
Because I understand
I understand what it's like to feel the hands of failure grip
    your excellence by its collar and intimidate the greatness
    out of you

To be consumed of what you're supposed to do when you
    don't even know who you're supposed to be
You are not alone
We reside in the same empty house
Where fear hangs like curtains to keep your shine out
When you question if your shadow is a reminder of who
    everyone wants you to be
It still chases behind when you try running from it
I get it

But face yourself in the mirror and know that you are not
    made of sand

That your future doesn't stand in the hour glass of time
Know that clocks are only there to remind you that your heart
    still beats to the rhythm you measure your own success by

I've wanted to kill myself.

To die with the thoughts that questioned my existence
To lay in the box that people tried to keep me in
I almost let them win
Almost let them run the race of my journey to finding myself

People will try to Columbus you
Exploit your goods
Claim them as their own
Then leave you to suffer
Blame it on manifest destiny when it's your destiny that
    manifests only in you
Take back what's yours!
Life doesn't hand out lollipops
But it'll sure give you licks
Do you realize you were born to fight?
So square up with those fists
You have knuckles made from backs
The type that carried you through the storm

Looked it dead in its eye and even made hurricanes question
    its power
So you better not question yours!

Do you know that you are extraterrestrial?
You were born to shoot for the stars so I hope you stay
    strapped
To live in space where gravity can't even hold you down

Do you know you were supposed to be an assassin?
To kill the game and destroy every hating target that tries to
    shoot you down

It's funny
People will teach you to be nonviolent
To be silent and passive
But closed mouths don't get fed so show me what you're
    hungry for
I'll show you my hands calloused from pushing myself
I'll show you my heart bruised but not broken

There are days where I've felt at my lowest
Thinking the price of success was at the expense of my soul
I used to drown in my own misery

I used to drink out of control
But I'm tired of taking shots at myself
It's time to sober up

Stop measuring yourself to the standards of others 'cause you
    are likely to get fooled
You've got to stay prayed up 'cause the devil will happily skip
    you to your tomb
Stones are meant for building and not throwing
So stop casting them at yourself
You've got so much to be thankful for
At least you can breathe
At least you're not dead
At least you have shoulders that holds up a good head
Start giving yourself the credit you deserve

It's easy to let failure bully you
But let your success be your hero

I cried while writing this poem
I promise you're not doing as bad as you think you are
Trust me when I say that you're not alone
But I promise this
We will get through this together
Once you realize the greatness that you hold

June 17, 2015 (Charleston)

I wish I could just *live*.
Just *be*.
Just *love*.
I constantly tell myself:

> *"Raising a black boy is going to be hard!*
> *Wait, no.*
> *Raising a black girl will be harder!*
> *C'mon, be real.*
> *A black boy will be much more exhausting.*
> *No, no, no.*
> *A black girl will be much worst, for sure."*

But I realize
Raising a *black child* is going to be difficult.
So what is a mother to do when she can't even explain her
   own existence?
To defend life when waking up every day is a battle already
   lost
To create a happy ending when we know how the story really
   ends

My children
I've feared for you when you weren't even a thought
I may have to start planning your birthdays and funerals
I've picked out your first day of school and casket outfits
My children
I fear for you so much
But know that God is the only thing we can all hold on to

Hashtag Tired

My heart is so heavy
Tired of trying to keep myself together
Scared to look on Facebook
Scared to look on Instagram
Scared to look on Twitter
Tired of my timelines being protest
boards, graveyards and vigil sites
I'm so tired of being targeted
So tired of defending my people but getting
criticized for having a voice
So tired of new hashtags
So tired of praying over dead bodies
So tired of being tired
I'm just...tired of being...#tired

Have Mercy on the Poet
(22 years old)

To the people who want me to write poems about tragedies I
    am not ready to write about yet:
Have mercy on the poet who has no words
We marry melancholy and exhaustion in poetry everyday
We introduce them in metaphor and coerce them to flirt in
    figurative language
Engage hurt in stanzas and prepare the confetti
Bind grief within mouth as we spit funerals for snaps and
    mask them as weddings

When death is on our tongues
When dead bodies are in our pens
When ink blots are blood clots spilled on papered crime
    scenes we memorize like prayers
Who said it was safe to be a griot when we exploit stories that
    sound like urban remixes of CNN
We pen the stories of the deceased
But are paranoid that the police are in our rear views and
    notebooks

There are no body cameras on these pages to protect us from
the brutalities we report
It is unsafe to be a voice
To bear the burden of boldness
To be a David when Goliath growls at your confidence and
threatens to slay
Any bit of Beyoncé you have left in you

I stand in front of my television and cry
I stand in front of my computer and cry
But I'm expected to stand in front of an audience with no
tears and dried eyes
To conjure the courage to make the poem breed sorrow for me
and you

To form an opinion when Instagram is already forming it for
you
Producing poems at the same rate as hashtags
Social media needs a reaction more than we need time to
process what's actually going on
I cannot grieve faster than the protest you are organizing
tomorrow

I can't articulate my thoughts faster than the bullet going into
    the next black body
How many different ways can I write the same poem?
I'm pretty sure all I have to do is switch out the name
But I cannot switch off the emotional impact it has every time
    I hear of a new case

Have mercy on the poet who has no words
The irony is that as poets, sometimes we just have no words
It's easy to become numb by time
But we have to hang on to any last bit of emotion so we can
    use it down the line
So we can have the strength to write again, process, and
    practice self-care

To the people who want me to write poems about tragedies I
    am not ready to write about yet,
Have mercy on the poet
Because as much as you need our art to fuel justice and
    morale
We need to make sure that we're well enough to do it

On Mizzou: Institutional Oppression
(22 years old)

I've tried being white before I've tried being myself
I've been taught to excuse my blackness before I've been
    taught to excuse my manners
To be mindful that my skin may cause people to be
    uncomfortable, so I should adjust accordingly
I almost didn't write this poem to accommodate your feelings

I believed my blackness was a disease only caught by those
    who deserved to be punished at random
But your institutions choose to subjugate my people in tandem
As if I was awaiting trial in my mother's womb, and my birth
    was a life sentence to injustice

You say that institutional oppression doesn't exist
Like it's a Santa Clause of some sort
But even your St. Nick can break into homes at night for your
  children
And you still leave him cookies while he does the job!
Meanwhile
We get shot for buying skittles and drinking ice tea
Or raising our hands up when we've surrendered our dignity
  to your oppression centuries ago

We stood in solidarity long before you stood for our rights
Jim Crow never flew away
Just nested in your laws

Diversity week in my school is not good enough to meet your
  quota of inclusion
You only give me a month where you have to tolerate my
  blackness
In the human race, your privilege gives you a head start
Yet you treat affirmative action like a consolation prize that
  we didn't deserve

Mr. President of Mizzou

Tim Wolf

Don't act surprised that your students are acting like animals
    in your Miz-zoo of an institution

America

Don't act surprise that your black citizens have reached their
    boiling point in this "melting pot" of a country

I'm sorry for making you uncomfortable with words like
    "racism" and "oppression"

But I've been uncomfortable with your actions

Genocide is starting to look like law enforcement

Red, white and blue is in inequality's kaleidoscope

Black people can't just be dope, without having you add
    dealer to the end of it

At a predominately white institution I have to worry about
    passing exams and passing as a good Negro

It's 2015

And I've only wanted to sit at your table that my ancestors
    cleaned for you

I never wanted to write another race or oppression poem
Another angry poem
Another remember my struggle poem
You must be exhausted hearing them, right?
But imagine how exhausting it is to live it everyday

You say that institutional oppression doesn't exist
But try unpacking your invisible knapsack and acknowledge
    the weight that I carry
Unveil your blinders because I'm tired of being invisible
Tired of being divisible

This is not your fault

But if we keep ignoring this fairy tale
We call our reality
I'm afraid that both our stories will never see a happy ending

Identity Part 6: Reconciliation

I'm growing to reconcile all of my different identities.

Burnt

[burnt]

Verb

1. ~~Simple past tense and past participle of burn.~~

Adjective

2. ~~Of or showing colors having a deeper or grayer hue than is usually associated with them.~~

Burn

[burn]

Verb (used without object), burned or burnt, burning.

1. ~~To undergo rapid combustion or consume fuel in such a way as to give off heat, gases, and, usually, light; be on fire.~~
2. ~~To feel heat or a physiologically similar sensation;~~ **to feel pain** ~~from or as if from a fire.~~
3. ~~To give off light or to glow brightly.~~
4. ~~To give off heat or be hot.~~
5. **To love and be loved.**
6. **To injure, endanger, or damage** ~~with or as if with fire.~~

Burnt [burnt]
Verb.

To feel pain. To love and be loved. To injure, endanger, or damage.

Would it Freak You Out

Would it freak you out if I told you
That I think about you
No less than 100 times a day?
I've seen your silhouette in my bacon
Which makes me look forward to breakfast every morning
I've stalked your Facebook profile, thoroughly
I knew you before I knew you
But I still act surprised when you tell me something "new"
I hum to the rhythm of your heartbeat
I measure time by the times I've made you laugh
I practice my jokes before I tell them to you
And even when they're not funny,
You still chuckle anyway
I've seen your smile in galaxies
I've heard your voice in symphonies
I've smelled your scent in carnations
I've tasted your sweetness in sugarplums
I've felt your warmth in my grandmother's quilt
Does this freak you out?
Good.
Freaks me out, too
Because I've never experienced love
Until I met you

Acrophobia

I hate looking up to kiss you
Mice can't be giraffes
Cottages can't be skyscrapers
But I'd take stairs to reach your lips
I'd hike your Everest to reach the top of your eyes
Just to say I've seen heaven before
It looks like smoked almonds painted in last night's
    eyeshadow
Feet turned ballerina
With an arch curved like your hips
I tippy toe toward tasting time in your tongue
I am no longer afraid of heights

You hate looking down to kiss me
Giraffes can't be mice
Skyscrapers can't be cottages
But you'd take the long way home,
Down the hill to reach my lips
You'd jump out of planes to skydive toward my eyes
Just to say you've reached Nirvana before
It looks like mustard seeds painted in last night's mascara
Back turned contortionist
With a curve rounded like my hips
You bow to behold my beauty bottled in bouquets of bliss
You are no longer afraid to fall

On Thinking Too Hard in a Relationship if You're Not Sure if They're Into You as Much as You're Into Them

Girl.
Relax.

Trophies
(20 years old)

I've loved one before
But love's never won before
I kept tying with this girl and that girl
So I guess that made us all winners in your world

We all became your trophies.

We shared you like pie
Like secrets
Like thoughts
Like friends
Were silly hoes to your pimp walk
The laughing stock of the game
But we took it like real trophies did
Our statures stood aesthetically astounding as we stood
    stoically stupid
Reflected your smile when you'd admire our beauty that
    glowed with pride
Rusted us by the minute when you showed us off from behind
But they ain't got no award for looking foolish in the public eye
Unless you count judgment as a consolation prize

But I thought I was the only star in your galaxy.

I was willing to breast feed our unborn son just to be a part of
    your milky way
I'd take a Train to catch the Drops of Jupiter in my palm
I'd sing songs while I stitched your black holes into colored
    pockets
Shit, I even paid attention to your big bang theories of
    craziness

I never knew this was coming.

Although I was one of your trophies you only polished me on
    occasion
Didn't know I wasn't your prized possession
Didn't know I volunteered to be flaunted every blue moon
Had us in rotation like the phases of the moon
I figured one of your trophies to be your crescent
Ya know, since heifers jumped over them of course
But why buy the cow when you're getting the milk for free
I figured your other trophy to be your quarter
    since she was only worth a quarter of your time
And I became your waning gibbous with your love almost but
    never fully there
Together we were your full moon

But only one third of your ideal woman
Only a figure to be flaunted when you wanted to see a new
    figure

But I never figured out why I was okay with being a trophy
Why we were okay with sitting on the dusty shelves of our
    self-esteem
Waiting to get picked up and deemed valuable for the moment
The Real MVP lies within us
I had to wake up from this fairytale you shook me out of years
    ago
Yea it's hard to let fears go
Too stubborn to admit that you, my prince charming didn't
    exist
That I could never be your queen sovereign
But only just your petty object
Your trophy
Your momentary love
I've loved one before
But they ain't got no award for that

Trophies.

Read 4:02 am

I hold on to every text message you send me
We connect through keyboards
I know this alphabet spells I love you somewhere
Just waiting for your fingers to catch up with my heart
Glued to my phone at night
I hold it imagining it to be your hand
Right now
I can't give you the world
Or flowers
Or a car
But will you accept them in emojis, instead?
I've been reluctant to memorize your number
I'm afraid to dial the amount of how much you mean to me
For only your answering machine to receive it
I've heard your voice in my inbox
It lingers in our conversation thread
It sews my feelings into patterns my tongue fails to create in
words
I write text messages
As electronic love letters
But I only ask that you don't take eternity to reply
Delivered

Used (Stranger)
(18 years old)

I opened my vagina to a stranger who knew its walls too well
Squeezed, sucked and stroked a forbidden territory he easily
    slid his hands and tongue through
Looked at my Sistine Chapel like amateur artwork without the
    potential of ever becoming a masterpiece
My pride found no peace but his pride found home in his
    pants
Maybe if pride was swallowed we could both call a truss
But no use
I just swallowed his pride with no hands

Men have used women like toilet seats
Claim them to be on the throne
Then do their business and such
He called me a queen and I blushed
But it wasn't because I was worthy, it was because I was
    convenient
A load of shit I won't forget to flush

Sorry if this sounds bitter but I'm writing to how he tasted
Sorry if this sounds hurtful but I'm writing to how it felt
    afterwards

He'd tell me,
"Baby, "you're fucking amazing"
Or,
"Baby, fucking you is amazing"
But baby
Am I really amazing or is it just the fucking part?
It hurt afterwards but I wondered if he hurt me on purpose
My body answered by writing a letter to my uterus that signed
    "guilty and gullible" in cursive
    Getting screwed will only screw you over if love is not
present in the fine print of my vagina's contract, period.
Maybe it was luck
But God granted me with a statement that did not mention a
    baby and ended in a period
But there are periods when I wonder if blood is really a
    reward or punishment

Maybe if Wal-Mart sold chastity belts we could stop sagging
    our dignity and pull our panties back up
Maybe young girls wouldn't spread like peanut butter then
    feel like jelly afterward
Maybe he'd recognize me as a fierce feminine feline instead
    of walking pussy
Actually talk to me instead of con-versing

Conning verses from a players bible but I continue to sing his
     hymns because they sound so sweet
But to him…
I'm just another holy *ghost* of a girlfriend only called upon to
     hear me shout to God as he enters my gates to heaven
While I put myself through hell for him
Offering my vagina in a tithing envelope just to be
Licked
Collected
Then counted
I was baptized in his hair but now he is knotted in my mind
If only he practiced what he preaches half of the time I
     wouldn't feel like such a heathen?
But how could he even make a sin feel so good?
All he did was hide behind some latex and left no prints of
     ever being there

Pain can be measured by a broken heart
So open my chest and arrest this stranger for breaking and
     entering
Because I don't know our men
Anymore.

Summer Fling

You, my favorite
Season. Passion dripped like sweat.
Melted my ice cream

Hey.

Hey_____, it's Shelby and I just….
(Deletes)

Hey_____! I'm reaching out to say hello. It's Shelby, btw lol. It's been a while since we last spoke and the conversation ended abruptly. Just wanted to make sure that we're still good…
(Deletes)

Hey_____, hopefully you haven't deleted my number. It's been a while since we last spoke. Just reaching out to see how you're doing….
(Deletes)

Hey_____, I hope things are going well for you….
(Deletes)

Hey_____, um…I miss you…
(Deletes)

Hey_____, I'm sorry….
(Deletes)

Hey_____, I still love you…
(Deletes)

Hey.
(Sends)

Nostalgia
(17 years old)

Your taste still lingers on my lips after I kiss my new
    boyfriend each night
So smooth your Nivea lip chap on mine and let our lips chat
    like old times
I mean, damn
Your scent is stained in the concaves of my nostrils and I can't
    smell the difference between you and him unless I open
    my eyes
I didn't think moving on would take so much time
I'd waste my time thinking about you
I remember the hold you had on my waist as our fingers
    intertwined a time or two
You used your finger a time or two
To point our love in the right direction

You journeyed my Atlantis and got lost in my Sahara
Climbed my Eifel tower and admired my Giza
Leaned on my tower of Pisa and enjoyed the view so much
    you extended your visa
Walked along my great walls and Niagara'd my Falls
But in all

I don't recall doing the same for you
I swear you will always be my Nostalgia dipped in sweet
honey and nectar
Glazed with the memories of our high school days
But as much as I want this ship to sail
Your oceans swallow me back into your belly
And anchor me back to the idea of us trying it again

I see that you're still hesitant to try it with me again
I understand that desperation leads to dismay and love poems
leads to clichés
But wrapping this ink into the lines of this page is the closest
I'll ever be to wrapping my arms around you again

I try to think about *him* to distract me from *you*
A dream come true
But a nightmare awake is called the real world and in it
It's hard dreaming with a broken heart when the figment isn't
infinite
Maybe he putting me to sleep will help me wake up easier
But nostalgia is insomnia without the diagnosis and there are
no doses of pills for me to take
Just repeating habits that are hard to break

And I can't put you to rest because these memories keep me
    up 'til dawn's break
Were the dreams we had fake?
Or is fate just using me as target practice
Because I hate not being able to state that I am okay without
    you

And I know you don't want me
And I know I can't want you
And I know you've moved on
And I want to move on, too

But…damn…

Let cherry blossoms trail unto a sidewalk of moving forward
Let gazelles prance on my smile as I approach a new love
Let family dance and cheer as I walk down the aisle to my
    eternity

But currently

Your taste still lingers on my lips after I kiss my new
    boyfriend each night
And I'm waiting
Still waiting
To try something new

To The Homie I Had No Business Loving

I'm writing to you because I'm confused. Heartbroken. Lost.
There's a lingering sense of disappointment when I'm around
you. I don't know how to make sense of these feelings. To be
torn between lover and homie, and having to choose *just* one.
Overtime, they became impossible to co-exist. Maybe it was
the poetry. I heard somewhere that poets can't be in love with
each other. We're some of the most troubled, tormented and
distressed people in this world. Yet, our pain is our genius. We
love hard and hurt harder. You inevitably became the source
of my brilliance.

I hate ignoring you. I hate this hesitation of reaching out to
you. I hate thinking of you in ways that are exaggerated and
untrue. At times, I miss being your homie. I miss just kickin'
it. When we would spend hours on the phone or in your room
talking shit about life, or doing absolutely nothing while
sitting comfortably in silence; When I called you at night so
I wouldn't feel lonely on my drive back home; When I was

able to call on you whenever I needed someone for a source of strength; For support; For a shoulder; For an ear. We would get lost in our daydreams of poetry and bask in thoughts of becoming the people we always wanted to be. We were two lost souls that found solace in each other. We were navigating our way through life - even though we had no idea where the hell we were going. We found comfort in the fact that we were figuring it out together. I guess in those moments I was only just a homie to you. But in those moments, you were always a lover to me.

You may read this and think that I'm crazy. You may even feel guilty because your intentions were never meant for me to love you much as I do. You may feel nothing right now. But understand that you've etched your name in my heart, time capsuled our memories in my soul and buried your love in a place that I have no business visiting ever again. Comfort zones and friend zones have one thing in common - it's a hard place to leave. I tried to escape both, but I knew I had no business trying. I ended up right back in this moment - knowing that lover and homie are impossible to co-exist when I'm with you.

When I Was Your Earth
(21 years old)

I remember when I was your earth
And you dug me
Yea, you really dug me
You dug my terrain
You dug my soil
You dug my flowers
And I was digging you too

But it was no surprise you were a hoe.

And I, your earth
Surface you penetrated
Dug into land that past gardeners abandoned long ago
You loved to dig in me
But never to my roots because that was too deep for you
Your stick didn't extend long enough
But you were never good at laying down wood anyway

My roots were too deep for you?
You buried our issues there
But instead of getting to the root of the problem you uprooted
    yo ass out of the situation

You loved diggin' through me
Only to generify but never rectify my garden although you
    loved playing in it
I bet you know what roses really smell like
My shit started to stink when I met you
My grass was greener before I met you
Maybe it was the pesticide you used to kill any type of
    commitment I placed upon you
That must've bugged you, didn't it?

You loved digging through me
But you plowed your way around my heart
Don't you know I be Mother Nature?
I produced the crops you tried to *eat* last night
Not even your rain dance can get me wetter than the tides I
    raise in my own oceans
Don't you know I be Mother Nature
And it's my winds that made you cum to me
Over
And over
And over
And over again
Made you moan for my morning dew and sip on my nectar
    when you were parched
I knew yo ass was thirsty

And I quenched it every time although you dehydrated my
    love
Exploited the fruits of my labor I put into this earth to
    gardener relationship
But Mr. Gardner, don't you know I sustain your life?
I be air
I be photosynthesis, respiration, and transpiration
Which means
You function off me
Which means
You need to be careful if you refuse to nurture this
    relationship,
Because you could die without me

Man, you sure loved diggin' through me
And you dug me out until you dug up my entire existence
Plucked my petunias
Destroyed my dandelions
Killed my carnations
Severed my sunflowers
You exhausted all of my resources, although I gave you
    everything you needed to survive
Did I bloom prematurely?

Or maybe you just couldn't tend to my tethered pedals
It was my nature versus your torture
Ya know, we almost made new land
You, my captain planet and I, your Good Earth
We almost made sky
We almost made space
Just to show that this love had no limits
More than what gravity could hold down
We almost suffocated air
We almost split seas
We almost split trees
Molecules, atoms/Adams and Eve
But you can keep your shovels
You only used them to dig graves and bury any chance of us
    becoming the eighth world wonder

I remember when I was your earth
And you dug me
Yea, you really dug me
But couldn't love me
And I'm waiting
To be restored back to life.

Coffee
(22 Years Old)

We were supposed to get coffee today
To kick it over creamer and caramel
Create dreams that kept our minds spinning like carousels and
    trampoline across skies as we bounced 'round clouds from
    our caffeine high

I was craving your coffee
But instead you'd rather sip on tea since our relationship was
    so full of it
Shared secrets I thought dissolved in your trust like packs of
    sugar dissolving in your cups
You were the first person to see that I had a little sugar in my
    tank
Because I was sweet on you
A woman
Beautiful in your glory
Smooth like milk as you poured passion in my mug
Strong and black like decaf
Whipped me like cream
And I stood eager in your line every morning because you
    were the best part of waking up

My Nestle and Folgers
Scorched my throat as I drank from your Keurig while kissing
    on your neck and shoulders
Your lattes had me like singing lat-tee da-tee daaaa
'til you realized ...
This love required a lat-tee work that you weren't willing to
    grind for
Sorta like coffee beans grinded by Brazilian slaved hand

Let us never forget
We coffee drinkers conditioned to numb our tongues from
    tasting their labor as they stripped their lands for a
    freedom they'd never see
We conditioned our tongues to only taste the benefits of their
    labor as they stripped their lands for freedom they'd never
    see
Now let us see
You conditioned to numb your tongue from tasting my labor
    as I stripped my dignity for a commitment I'd never see
You conditioned your tongue to only taste the benefits of my
    labor as I stripped my dignity for a commitment I'd never see

You see how you juxtapose?
I suppose I had no business wanting you
Since you made it your business to profit off my love

Gave you my Café con leche with no return on your
    investment
Bankrupted my trust and wasted all my time I spent on you
We both failed to see the margin of error before becoming
    partners

You see
We were supposed to get coffee today
Spend bucks at Starbucks or sip somethin' at Dunkin'
But was I craving the caffeine or was I craving you?
Blurring the lines between desire and addiction
Purposely taking these shots
Of expresso
For you
In hopes
That you'd finally wake the fuck up to a good thing that
    looked a lot like me
Your heart
Iced like macchiatos
I learned that drinking coffee is only a temporary high
How it excites you for a few hours only to get tired as the day
    progressed
Like the course of our relationship
Like how I thought you were the perfect blend of creativity
    and mocha

And how baristas grew jealous because they couldn't make
    coffee look and taste as good as you
But your heart was iced like macchiatos
Like how you grew colder and distant by the day
Even when I tried to warm your soul with my cappuccino'd
    love I brewed especially for you
You preferred the chai
You really preferred the chai
Rather than giving us a try
And I thought you really loved me
Like how I thought I was writing a poem about coffee
Like how I was ready to fall back in love the same way you
    fell out of it
Over a momentary feeling that quietly faded as the day went on
Sorta like coffee.

I read somewhere that tea is actually better for you anyway
It's natural
Like our connection
But unlike our willingness to work it out
Maybe one day we'll wake up to find love staring across the
    table
But for now,
Let's reschedule to meet up another time.